1001 SCROLLS, ORNAMENTS AND BORDERS

READY-TO-USE ILLUSTRATIONS FOR DECOUPAGE AND OTHER CRAFTS

Edited by
Eleanor Hasbrouck Rawlings

Dover Publications, Inc.
New York

Published in Canada by General Publishing Company, Ltd., 30 Lesmill Road, Don Mills, Toronto, Ontario.
Published in the United Kingdom by Constable and Company, Ltd., 10 Orange Street, London WC2H 7EG.

1001 Scrolls, Ornaments and Borders: Ready-to-Use Illustrations for Decoupage and Other Crafts is a new work, first published by Dover Publications, Inc., in 1979. The designs have been selected by Eleanor Hasbrouck Rawlings from Catalogue "K," *Period Carvings*, of the Syracuse Ornamental Company, Syracuse, New York, 1923. Mrs. Rawlings has also written a new Introduction especially for this Dover edition.

DOVER *Pictorial Archive* SERIES

1001 Scrolls, Ornaments and Borders: Ready-to-Use Illustrations for Decoupage and Other Crafts belongs to the Dover Pictorial Archive Series. Up to ten illustrations from this book may be reproduced on any one project or in any single publication free and without special permission. Wherever possible please include a credit line indicating the title of this book, author and publisher. Please address the publisher for permission to make more extensive use of illustrations in this book than that authorized above.
The republication of this book in whole is prohibited.

International Standard Book Number: 0-486-23795-8
Library of Congress Catalog Card Number: 78-75363

Manufactured in the United States of America
Dover Publications, Inc.
180 Varick Street
New York, N.Y. 10014

INTRODUCTION

The source of all the designs in this collection is the impressive catalogue issued in 1923 by the Syracuse Ornamental Company of Syracuse, New York, manufacturer of Syroco fibre wood units for moldings, panels, ceilings and other decorative purposes. The large-format 380-page salesman's aid contained thousands of beautifully rendered illustrations showing borders, scrolls, swags, trophees, garlands, cornucopias and other motifs in many period styles, such as Medieval, Renaissance, Baroque, Rococo, Chippendale, Adam, Louis XIV and Victorian. Rattling around the countryside in their Model T's, the busy salesmen probably never dreamed that the catalogue they used daily to sell their products to carpenters and architects would one day come to be recognized as a treasure trove of designs for craftwork of all kinds, but particularly for decoupage.

The present volume, which contains my personal selection of the most attractive designs for craft purposes, will appeal strongly to *découpeurs* because of the delicate shading which gives depth and dimension to the motifs, and because many appear also as reversed images, often in several different sizes. Moreover, the artwork is printed on one side of the page only, and on paper of a weight and texture that is especially appropriate for decoupage.

These designs are suitable for decoupage projects made of wood, metal, papier-mâché, ceramics, glass and even some plastics. Some suggestions:

Jewelry—earrings, pendants, bracelets, brooches.
Boxes of all shapes, sizes and materials.
Furniture—from small tables to tall secretaries.
Mirrors, wastebaskets, napkin rings, hand mirrors, picture frames, switch plates, trays.
Door frames, wall panels, screens, plaques, mantels.
Lamps, shades, urns, vases, ashtrays, ornamental plates.
Basket purses, box purses, picnic baskets, mailboxes.
Desk accessories, album covers, bookends, cachepots, paperweights.
Wig stands, driftwood, weathered wood, and so forth.

If it has a smooth surface you probably can decoupage it!

HOW TO OBTAIN MULTIPLE COPIES

Materials

Xerox machine (at your local library or photoduplication service).
Straight scissors.
Can of rubber cement (read the directions).

This collection contains several copies of some of the narrower borders and smaller designs, but lack of space prohibits duplication of larger units. These can be made easily on a Xerox duplicating machine. (Be sure it's a Xerox copier; most of the other duplicators use a paper with a film that doesn't take oil-pencil coloring well.) If you need many copies of one design, you can save money by clever juggling of the copy sheets and by using scissors and rubber cement. Make one copy, then paste it down on a sheet next to the original. Xerox this sheet (which will give you two designs) and paste *it* next to the first two. Xerox this one. By repeating this process you can obtain 2, 4, 8, 16, 32 or 64 copies, as needed.

COLORING AND SEALING YOUR PRINTS

After selecting an object to be decorated and working out a design, you next color and seal the print or prints. Do not cut out a design until after you have finished coloring and sealing it.

Materials

Oil-base colored pencils (Prismacolor, Derwent or Colorama). Three shades (light, medium and dark) of each primary and secondary color, black, white, terra-cotta, yellow ochre, burnt umber, raw umber, pink, flesh, slate gray. Some extra colors you may wish to add are lemon yellow, scarlet lake, Colorama's madder red, Paris green, apple green, indigo, cerise, sepia, burnt carmine, vermilion, pale gray.
Pencil sharpener.
Soft pink eraser such as Eberhard's Pink Pearl.
Sealer materials—one coat of acrylic polymer emulsion (Liquitex, Aquatec or Hyplar) or clear acrylic sprays such as Krylon, Blair or Clear Coat (matte finish).
½" Poly sponge brush.

Before the development of color printing, all designs for decoupage were colored by hand. Even today most serious *découpeurs* prefer to do their own coloring. The designs in this book are reproduced in soft gray-black on white to be hand colored. Many can be used without any coloring, but they are much more dramatic if color is used, and have more vitality under varnish.

Good-quality colored pencils with an oil base are the most satisfactory medium for coloring prints. They are easy to manage, blend well and can be erased with a soft pink eraser.

A magazine resting on a tabletop is a firm enough surface on which to color and is not too hard, as bare wood or glass would be. Too hard a surface will make your coloring look scratchy.

If a print is too dark, erase it partially with a good pink eraser so that it will take the color better. If you dislike your coloring you can erase it and start over.

For decoupage under glass, pastel or subdued colors can be used; stronger hues are better under many coats of finish, which markedly tone down all color.

To achieve a sculptured or three-dimensional effect with your coloring you must indicate it with shadows and highlights as well as local color (the color an object really is). A delicate, feathery or small design limits the scope of your coloring, and two or at most three colors are usually sufficient. With a heavy Baroque design on a large scale, more colors can be introduced.

Study your design and determine which parts would be raised up and nearer to you, and which fall away and are therefore farther back. Generally speaking, the nearer parts in these designs should be brighter and lighter in color value while those parts farther away should be subdued or darker. Decide from which direction the light is coming. If, for example, it comes from overhead and the right, the darkest shadows will fall to the left and at the lower contours of the various parts of the design. Sometimes the shading of the print itself helps to determine the source of light and you can follow the shading lines as you color.

After selecting an object to be decorated and working out a design, one next seals the print or prints. Do not cut out a design until you have sealed it. A clear acrylic spray with a matte finish, such as Krylon, Blair or Clear-Coat can be used. It is more economical to paint the print with a sealer solution of equal parts of white shellac and denatured alcohol in 3″-square segments. (Never use outdated shellac; it blisters under varnish.) Blot the sealer off immediately with Kleenex. Sealing prevents the colors from running and reinforces the paper for cutting and pasting.

The Grisaille Color Scheme

Grisaille is a monochromatic color scheme using shades of black, gray and white to produce the look of carved marble or plaster. It is often seen in Empire decor or on the rich gray-blue of a Wedgwood plate.

Start on the left side of the detail to be colored with the black pencil. Color very lightly about one fifth of the area, following the outside contours, slanting to (but not scratching across) lines. Continue on the lower edges. Use short uneven strokes, which blend better for an allover cover. Then, even narrower and more lightly, go down the right sides of the design and on the upper edges. Remember to sharpen your pencils often; your coloring must be precise.

With the slate gray pencil, very lightly and evenly color over half of the black (on the left and on the lower edges) and extend toward, but not to the middle of, the area. Always leave some white when you color and a highlight. The highlight can more or less follow the contours of the part of the design being colored. Color even more lightly on the right and upper edges of the design.

Now blend the colors with your white or pale gray pencil, following the contours, and without scratching across contour lines. Elyse Sommer, in *Decoupage Old and New*, suggests blending with a small piece of paper napkin on the point of your palest coloring pencil for that part of the design. Another method suggested by Dee Davis, of Adventures in Crafts, is to blend with the palest shade, leaving some white, of course. Don't make it look glassy and smeared. If you do, erase it and try again. Now go back with your black pencil and accent the shadows with a darker tone here and there. With a needle-sharp black pencil *very* delicately touch up some sections of the outlines, but not with continuous hard lines.

The techniques for the grisaille color scheme can be followed using other unifying colors of your choice.

The Gold Color Scheme

The gold palette is an analogous color scheme which may be used to produce the effect of a gilt metal decoration on furniture called "ormolu," or carved and gilded architectural details like those on frames, furniture, or buildings. Use raw umber or dark brown in the shadows, then terra-cotta with yellow ochre and/or lemon-yellow overlay, and palest yellow or white to blend all together. Sepia or darkest brown sharpened to a fine point can be used for accents and suggestion of outlines. The gold palette is handsome on black, white, green, blue and many other background colors.

The Sanguine Color Scheme

The sanguine palette might suggest carved pink sandstone. Use burnt umber for deepest shadows, shading into terra-cotta, scarlet lake and flesh. Flesh or white is used to blend all together. Backgrounds can be black, brown, gray, gray-blue, or a soft brownish-pink.

The Polychrome Color Scheme

A rich polychrome palette for Baroque scrolls and borders can use indigo blue in shadows, shading to ultramarine and to grass green in the heavier portions of the design. Lemon yellow can be introduced near the highlights and tips of the scrolls, with touches of pink on the very ends. Use white to blend all or pale blue, green or yellow, as indicated by the design. Touches of indigo accent the shadows. Black, white, gold and gray backgrounds are good choices.

The Chinoiserie Color Scheme

Chinoiserie can be rendered in many different color schemes, and if you are knowledgeable on this subject you will have no problems. If you're a beginner simplicity is advisable. The sanguine palette can be used throughout as in Katami ware, with brown, terra-cotta and vermilion—the orange-red colors dominating. A black, gold or white background is pleasing here.

Blue on white, as in Canton ware, is another choice that has a timeless appeal. Indigo blue in shadows shades into ultramarine and white.

The gold palette is still another possibility and is pleasing on a black, white, lacquer red or celadon green (a soft pastel grayish blue-green) background.

For a more colorful chinoiserie, take your dominant color scheme from a Chinese plate: blues (indigo blending to ultramarine and sky blue); orangy reds (terra-cotta blended with madder red and vermilion); green (Paris green, grass green, celadon green); golds (brown blended with terra-cotta, yellow ochre, lemon yellow). Backgrounds can be black, white, pale gold, lacquer red, celadon green, gold leaf.

CUTTING OUT YOUR PRINT

Materials

> Manicure scissors—good quality with fine, curved, sharp blades.
> Straight scissors to cut away excess paper.

Skillful cutting is a prime requisite for a fine piece of decoupage. First cut away all unnecessary paper for easier handling. If there are spindly parts that might break off, draw "ladders" to nearby points to reinforce them. These ladders are cut off just before you start to glue. Use colored pencils to thicken stems or lines that are too thin to cut, or eliminate them if they aren't essential.

If you are right-handed, hold the print in your left hand. Hold the manicure scissors in your right hand, with the curved blade pointing to the right and the palm of your right hand facing up, somewhat, as you cut. Feed the paper into the scissors with the left hand, turning the paper as you cut, rather than turning the scissors. Pulling the scissors and wiggling the paper slightly creates a minutely serrated and beveled edge, turned under that adheres well when glued.

Cut inside spaces first while there is more paper to hold onto when working. Poke a hole through from the top, then put the scissors up through the hole from the bottom; that way it's easier to see what you are doing. Eliminate unwanted details and backgrounds; silhouette the elements of the design.

Don't leave white edges or other evidence of careless cutting. If necessary, however, white edges *can* be touched up with a colored pencil. Very large prints should be cut into small segments, about 3″ square, and then be reassembled when gluing. The extra cuts will let air bubbles escape, hasten drying, and be especially helpful in molding flat paper prints to curved sufaces. Sometimes on a curved surface it may be necessary to allow a print to lie in a hot, damp towel and then to mold it gently in the palm of your hand so that it will fit perfectly. Occasionally, tiny, cleverly maneuvered slits will do the trick.

DECOUPAGE USING ACRYLICS

Among the recent wonder media for artists are the acrylics, versatile products which are particularly adaptable for decoupage and can bring the joy of creating in decoupage to children, the elderly or to handicapped persons.

Materials

> Acrylic polymer emulsion is sold under many trade names
>
> > Hyplar Gloss Medium and Varnish
> > Liquitex Gloss Medium
> > Aquatec Polymer Medium
> > Mod Podge
> > Regency Decoupage Finish
> > Cambridge Water-Base Decoupage Finish
> > decal-it

These finishes are water-soluble until they dry. They have no noxious odors, so allergy sufferers can use them, and they dry within an hour, making it possible to apply more coats in less time. They adhere to almost any non-oily surface including glass and plastics. They can be used as a sealer, a glue, a varnish and are tough and flexible enough to reinforce a cloth hinge on a box. They bind well to acrylic gesso or acrylic paints. They can be used to make a decal or transfer and are water-resistant. Many coats do not alter the colors as traditional varnish does. Varnish or lacquer can be applied over these acrylic polymers for a more permanent finish.

PREPARING YOUR BACKGROUND

Materials

> No. 220 garnet sandpaper.
> Small sanding block.
> Plastic wood to fill in holes, if any.

A hand mirror frame of wood or plastic becomes a conversation piece when elegantly decoupaged. Sand it lightly but thoroughly with No. 220 garnet sandpaper to provide a roughness for the background color to cling to, and smooth out rough spots or flaky paint.

PAINTING YOUR BACKGROUND

Materials

> Acrylic gesso (Liquitex, Aquatec or Hyplar).
> Acrylic paints in small tubes for tinting gesso a light shade if desired. For dark shades, Acrylic paints (in jars only) may be used. The white gesso will not take too much pigment.
> ½″ or 1″ poly sponge brush.
> Small bowl of water, detergent suds.
> Cloths.
> No. 320 Tri-m-ite paper (black, wet-and-dry sandpaper).
> Steel wool #0000.

The gesso should be about the consistency of cream. If brush marks show it's too thick, and you should thin it with a little water. Paint the back of the mirror frame and allow it to dry for about half an hour. Then paint the reverse side, carefully avoiding the mirror itself. When this has dried, a second coat should be applied with brush strokes at right angles to the first. A third coat, at right angles to the second, can be applied if necessary. Be sure to wash the brush thoroughly in water immediately after each coat. If the gesso hardens in the brush you may get it out, but the brush will never be the same—ditto rugs or your best sweater, so take care when using gesso.

The gesso must be "wet-sanded" next, with No. 320 Tri-m-ite paper dipped into detergent suds only, not water. After it has dried, polish it with #0000 steel wool to a velvety smoothness.

There are many other ways to finish the background, including wood stain, acrylic paints and gold leaf. Techniques for applying these are described in the reference books in the Bibliography.

GLUING

Materials

> Mucilage for decoupage (Harrower, Nimmock's or Mitchell).
> These dry slowly, so you can change your mind.

White glue (any good polyvinyl acetate glue such as Sobo or Elmer's) is a must for gold braid. These dry clear, but fast, so you can't change your mind. A few drops of Sobo or Elmer's in mucilage is helpful in sticking a print to a difficult surface.

X-acto knife.

Small sponges or pieces of old bath towel, paper towels, Kleenex, wax paper.

Bowl of water.

Paste brush, toothpicks, Q-Tips, corsage pin.

Apply the mucilage to the back of the print, and then apply the print carefully to the back of the mirror frame. Press down firmly but lightly, from the center out, with a barely damp sponge or piece of towel. (Wring it out until it is almost dry.) Try to press out excess glue or air bubbles, rolling your fingers as you go. Do not rub; this might damage your print or cause it to shift out of place. Press all edges down with your fingernail; hold the frame to the light to check that they are attached. Anything that sticks up will cause trouble later when you apply the finish. Take care of it now.

Allow the mirror to dry overnight. The next day check again for air bubbles. If you find any, slit them with the X-acto knife and apply Sobo glue. Probe all edges gently with the corsage pin and re-glue them if necessary. Check for shiny spots; they are glue and must be removed because glue or mucilage turns brown under the finish.

FINISHING

Materials

Good-quality, water-based decoupage finishes which take sanding well, such as Regency Decoupage Finish by Cunningham, Mod Podge (mat finish) by Brocado, Cambridge Water Based Decoupage Finish by Talisman.

½ or 1″ poly sponge brush.

Bowl of water.

Steel wool #0000.

Stir the finish gently so as not to stir up any air bubbles. Work in a dust-free room at a temperature of about 70° F (21.1° C).

Flow the milky finish on the back of the mirror frame with your brush as evenly as possible. Let it dry for an hour, or until it is perfectly clear. Turn it over and apply the finish to the mirror side. Continue this routine, *always* waiting until the finish is clear, until the design is submerged under the finish. Ten coats may be needed.

This would be a good place for children (whose attention span is short) to end their projects, also elderly, handicapped or allergic persons. If so, dry polish the mirror frame using 0000 steel wool with short circular strokes.

If your design is not submerged well enough to suit you after ten coats, apply five more, *always* waiting until the finish is perfectly clear.

SANDING

Materials

No. 400 Tri-m-ite (black, wet-and-dry sandpaper).

Bowl of water and detergent suds.

Damp sponge and towel.

Steel wool #0000.

Soft cloth.

Leave the edges and corners of the mirror frame until last or you may sand through the finish and create a troublesome repair job. Dip a 3″ × 2″ strip of the No. 400 Tri-m-ite paper into the suds and "wet-sand" over the top of the design to bring the level of the surface down to the level of the finish on the background. Wipe off any residue with the damp sponge or piece of towel. Don't sand all the way through to the print. If you do, touch up the spot with colored pencils to match. Then with emulsion on the tip of a brush apply 5 or more coats. Be more careful sanding that spot next time. Watch what you're doing.

Repeat the sanding process with No. 400 Tri-m-ite over the whole frame (except the edges and corners) taking down the finish more and obliterating any shiny spots. Continue until the finish is uniformly smooth, and no edges of the print can be felt.

FINAL COATS

Materials

Varnish—small quantity of good-quality semigloss, such as McCloskey's or Patricia Nimock's. 8oz. should be enough.

Turpentine (artist's quality) for thinning your varnish and cleaning your varnish brush only.

OR

Lacquer—a small quantity of good quality, such as Royal Coat Decoupage Finish by Cunningham or Deft by Deft. 8oz.

Lacquer thinner, for thinning lacquer and cleansing lacquer brush only.

No. 600 Tri-m-ite paper (black, wet-and-dry sandpaper).

½ or 1″ poly sponge brush.

Bowl of water and detergent suds.

Steel wool #0000.

White furniture wax, soft cloth.

Now apply several coats of decoupage varnish, waiting 24 hours between each coat. One can be applied in the morning on one side of the frame and on the other at night. Don't varnish on a rainy day or if the humidity is above 54%. After the final coat wait several days and then wet-sand with No. 600 Tri-m-ite paper and suds. The next step is to *dry*-polish the surfaces with #0000 steel wool, using a small circular motion. Gently polish the edges of the mirror frame with the steel wool, just enough to produce a soft, satin finish. Lastly, polish with a good white wax and a soft cloth.

If you are using lacquer as a final finish instead of varnish the three or four final coats can be applied, front and back, every hour, but *not* on rainy or humid days. Sand, polish and wax as above. Protect lacquer finishes from exposure to extremes of temperature or they will crack.

Let the mirror rest for a few weeks where there is good circulation of air (*never* in a cellophane bag) and there you are—triumphant. You can marvel at yourself and your artistry.

BIBLIOGRAPHY

For inspiration and instruction in various other techniques and finishes to enhance your creations, the following books are recommended. The definitive text is that of Mr. Hiram Manning of Boston, Massachusetts— *Manning on Decoupage.*

Davis, Dee and Dee Frenkel, *Decoupage, Step by Step*, Golden Press, 1976. Well illustrated, innovative.

Grotz, George, *The Furniture Doctor*, Doubleday, 1962. Still a favorite of those who have restored or wish to restore a piece of furniture.

Harrower, Dorothy, *Decoupage, a Limitless World in Decoration*, Crown Publishers, 1958. The first important book on decoupage to be published in the twentieth century describes decoupage and its antecedents, also collage and other related fields. Good reading.

Manning, Hiram, *Manning on Decoupage*, Dover Publications, 1980. The traditional method—blood, sweat and tears—but you'll have an heirloom, or a work of art, or both. Good reading, detailed instruction.

Mitchell, Marie, *Art of Decoupage* (manual), 1966, and *Advanced Decoupage* (manual), 1969. Clear and concise, follows traditional procedures.

Newman, Thelma R., *Contemporary Decoupage*, Crown, 1972. Covers history and traditional decoupage and has a whole chapter on decoupage on acrylic. Many innovations. Extensive sources of supply.

Nimocks, Patricia E., *Decoupage*, Scribner's, 1968. The chapters on coloring and cutting techniques are especially informative and helpful.

O'Neill, Isabel, *Art of the Painted Finish*, Morrow, 1971. A detailed study in this field, and a fine reference.

Sommer, Elyse, *Decoupage Old and New*, Watson Guptill, 1971. Mrs. Sommer appreciates fully the importance of traditional techniques and design in decoupage, but has stimulating new ideas, also. Good supply sources. Lesson plans for teachers.

Wing, Frances S., *Complete Book of Decoupage*, Coward McCann, 1965. Most of the emphasis is on the traditional approach. Mrs. Wing was among the first to recommend lacquer and plastic for speedy finishing and for objects receiving hard wear.

SOURCES OF SUPPLY

Adventures in Crafts, 1321 Madison Ave., New York, NY 10028. Studio for basic and advanced decoupage and collage. Instruction and supplies by appointment: (212) 410-9793. Mail order catalogue: $2.00, includes unusual and basic supplies, full color prints.

Craft Center, Gateway Shopping Center, Wayne, PA 19087. Wood, finishes, prints, books, hardware.

Creative Crafts, P.O. Box 700, Newton, NJ 07860. Bi-monthly crafts magazine, new products, techniques.

Dover Publications, Inc., 180 Varick St., New York, NY 10014. Free catalogue; extensive pictorial archive of sixteenth- to twentieth-century illustrations; mail order.

Harrower House, 37 Carpenter St., Box 502, Milford, NJ 08848. Gold Victorian trim, Pillimente prints, boxes, special Mucilage for Decoupage. Catalogue: $2.00, mail order, international.

Hazel Pearson Handicrafts, 16017 East Valley Blvd., City of Industry, CA 91744. Prints, supplies, catalogue, mail order.

Laffer Industries Inc., P.O. Box 335, Sandusky, OH 44870. Boxes of all kinds. Catalogue: $1.00, mail order.

The Manning Studio of Decoupage, 14 Wigglesworth St., Boston, MA 02120. Black-and-white prints only.

Plaid Enterprises, 6553 Warren Drive, Norcross, GA 30091. Royal Coat Lacquer and its techniques, manual, materials and prints, Regency Decoupage Finish.

Singerie, 1128 Larrabee St., West Hollywood, CA 90069. Black-and-white prints, supplies, instruction, Talisman, Cambridge Water-Based Decoupage Finish.

Your own attic; also garage sales, thrift shops, junk shops and flea markets for unusual objects.

The National Guild of Decoupeurs, 807 Rivard Blvd., Grosse Pointe, Mich. 48230, requires that its members meet rigid standards of excellence and artistry in order to be accepted. If you become a dedicated *découpeur* you may wish to join.

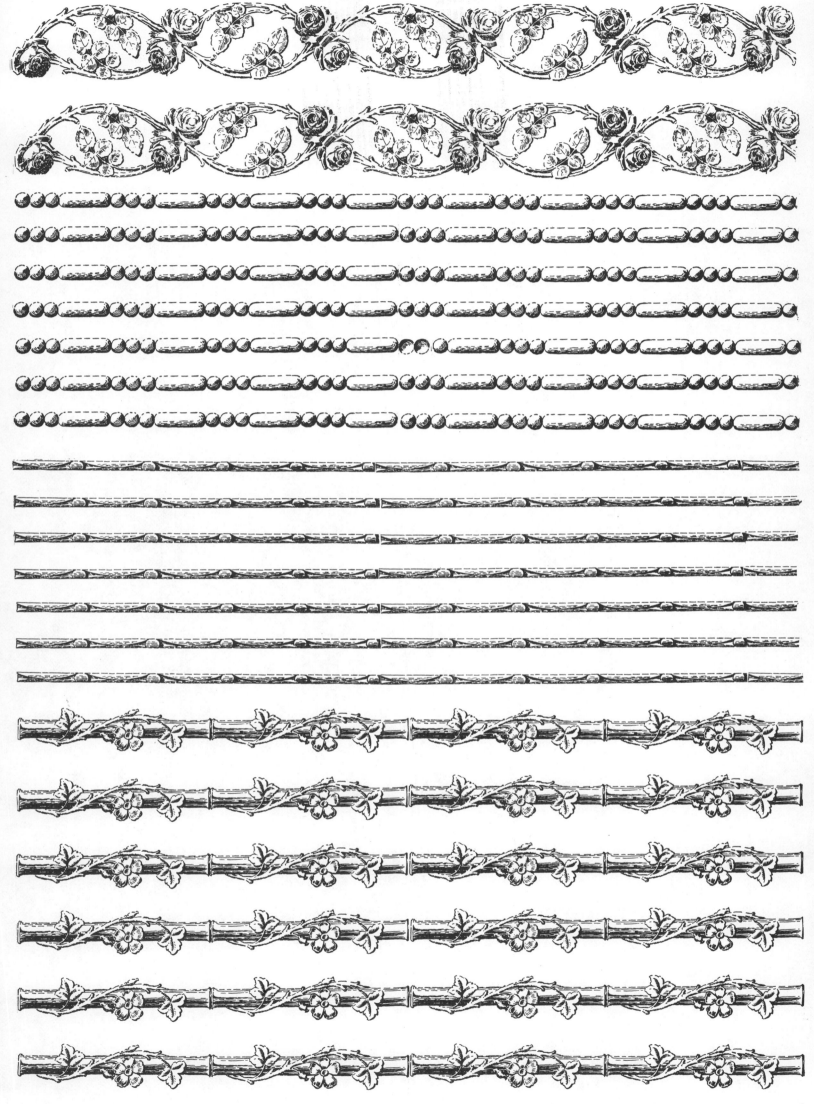

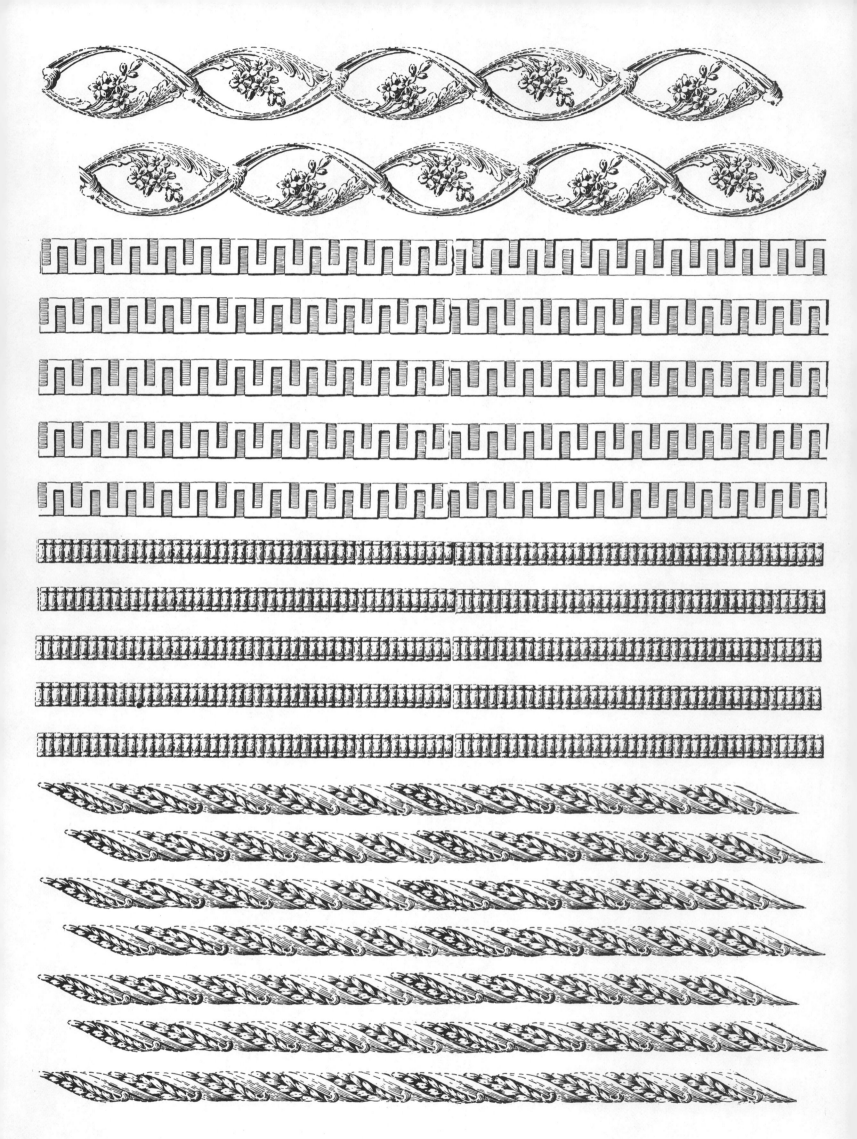

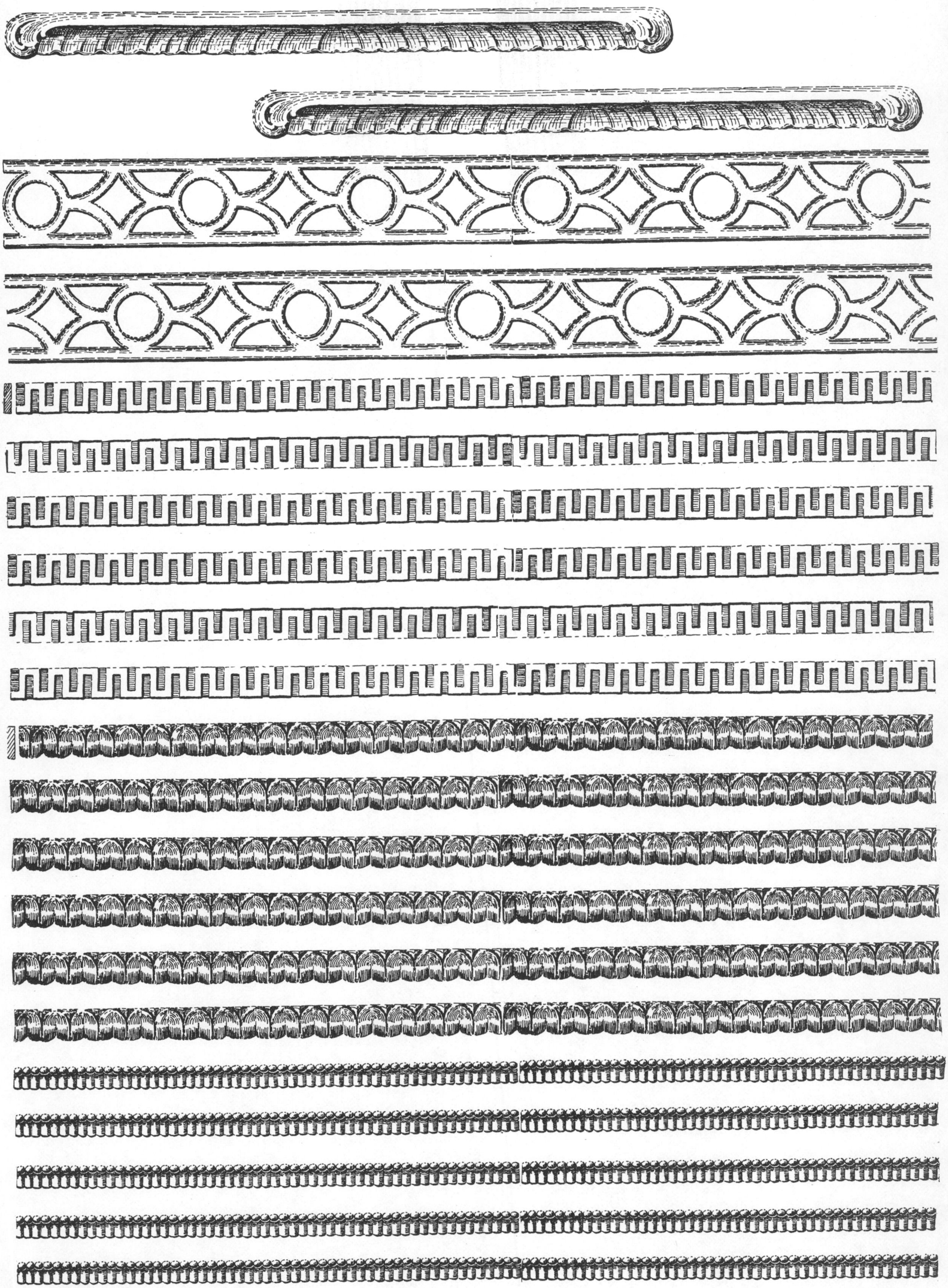

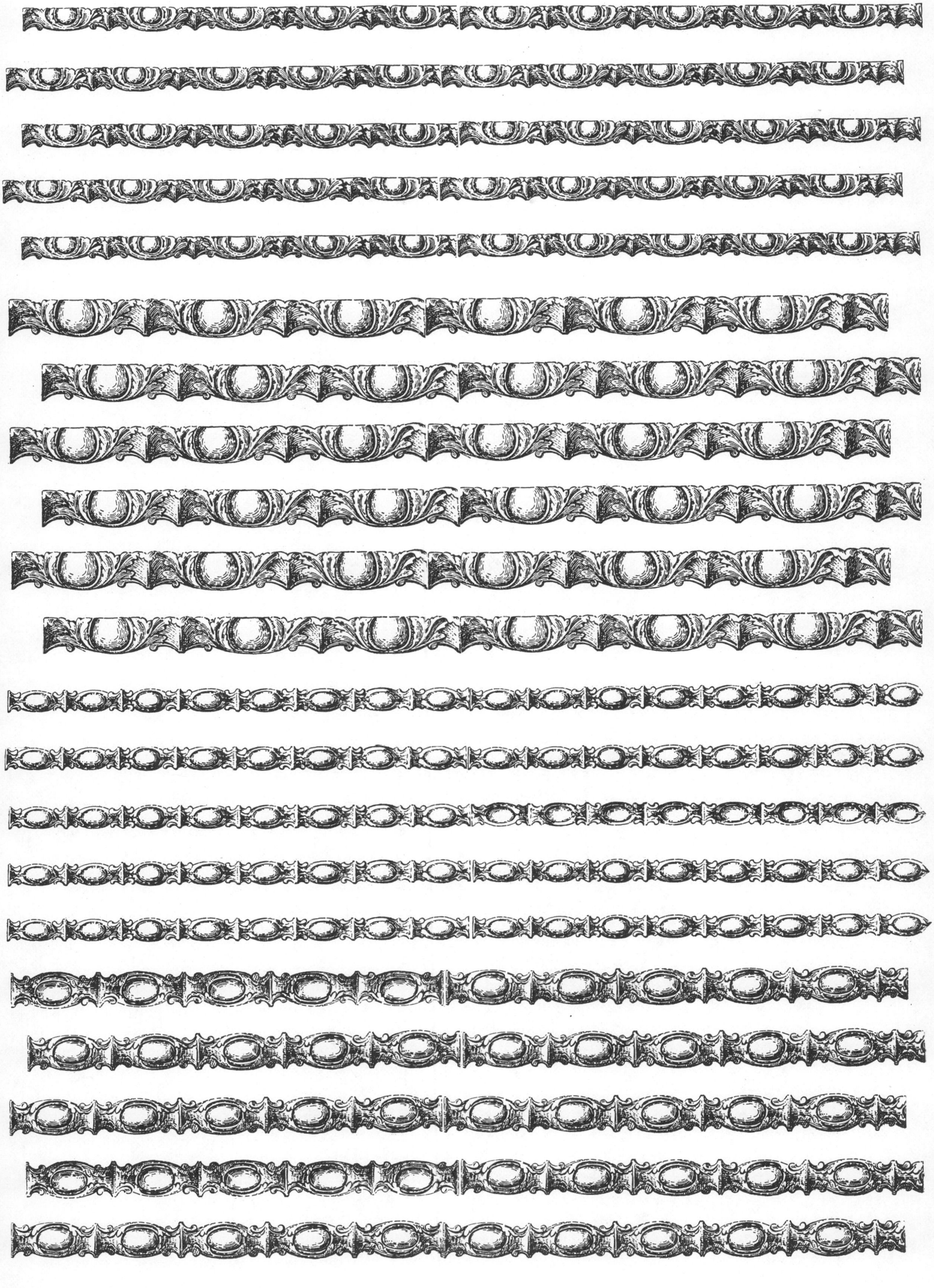

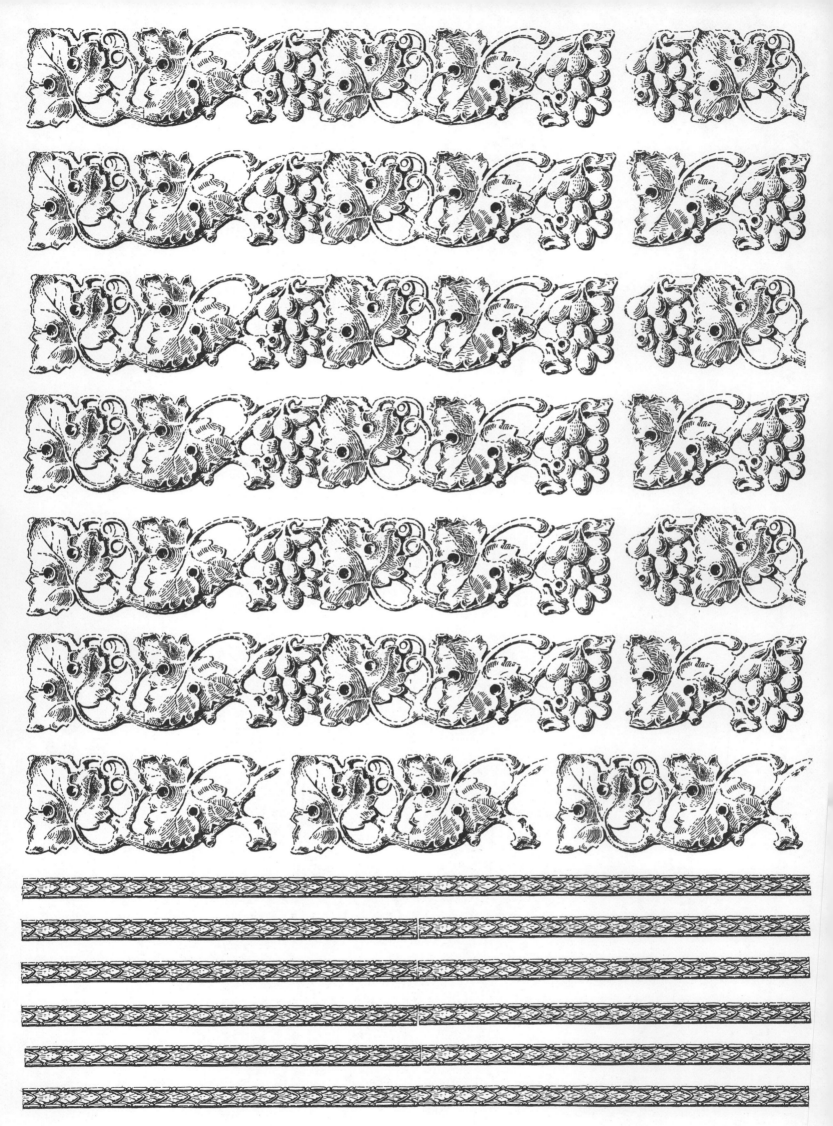

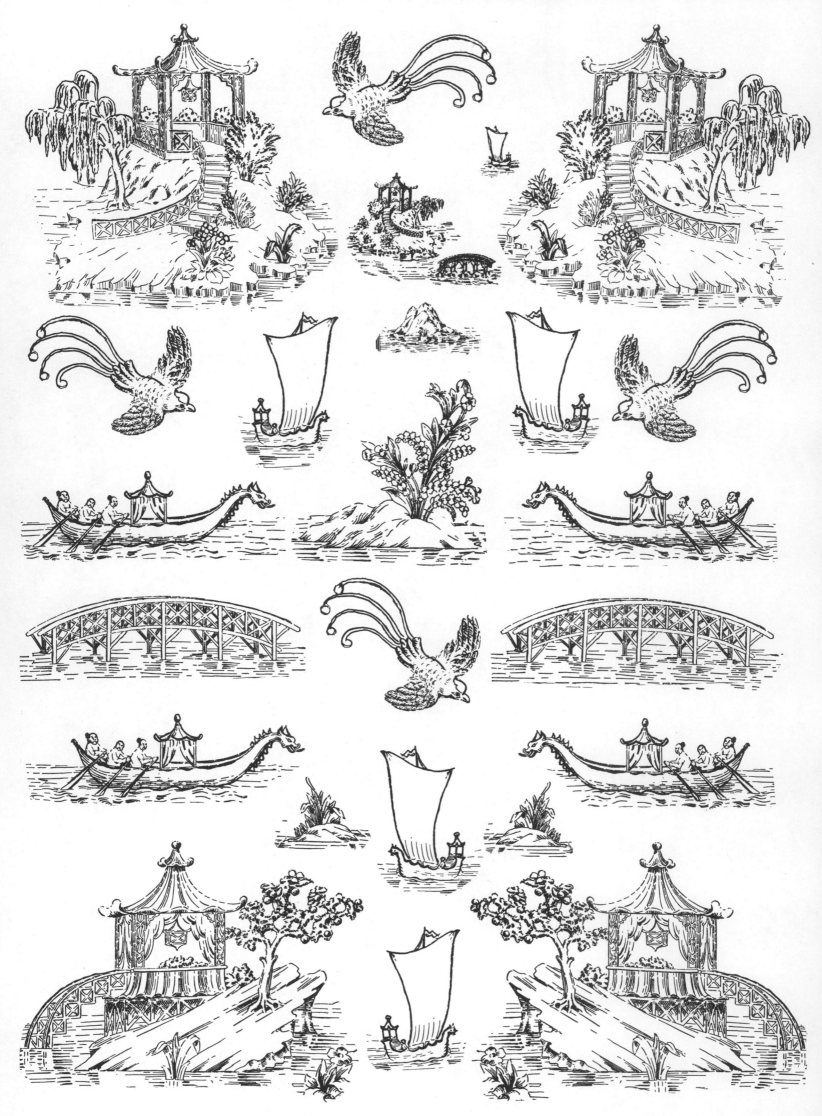

14

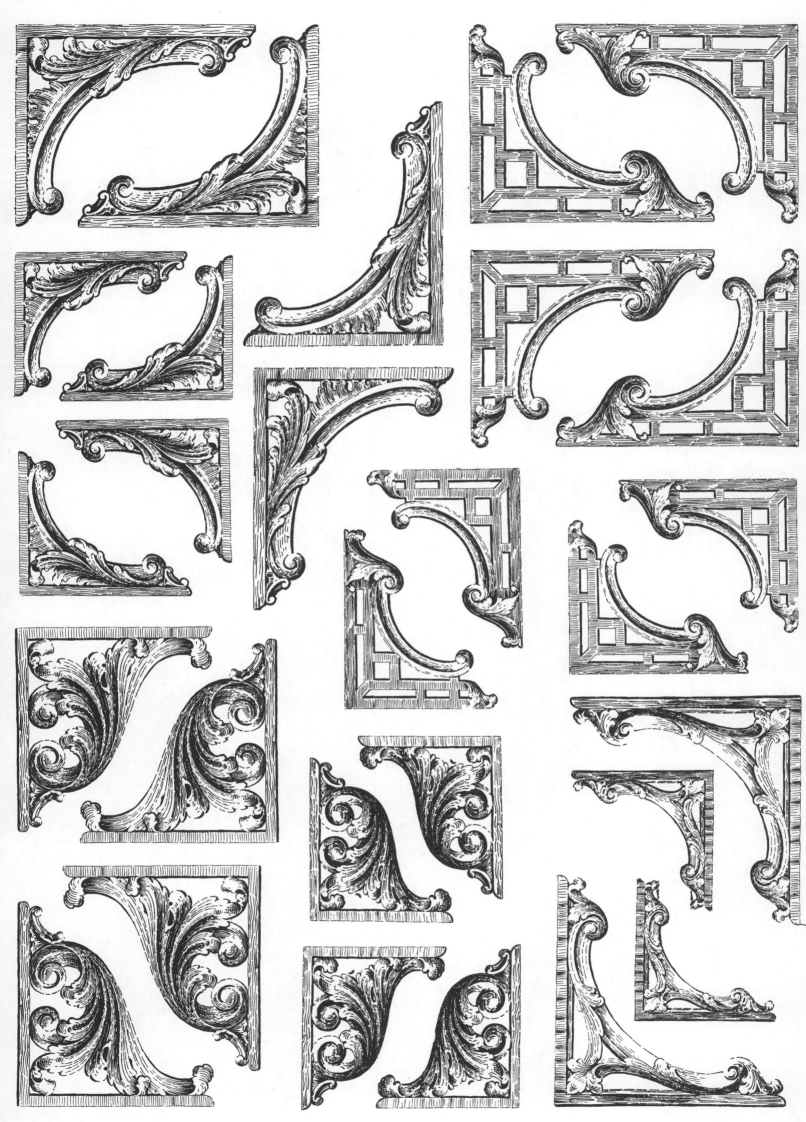

15

17

18

19

23

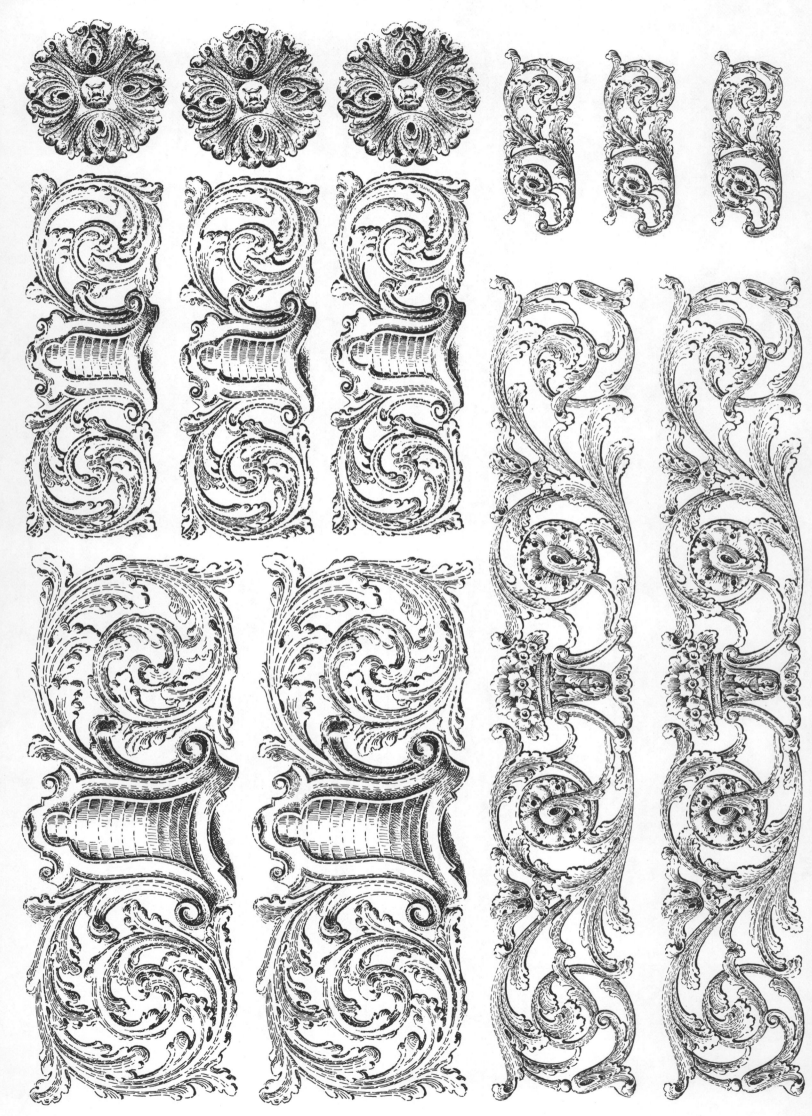

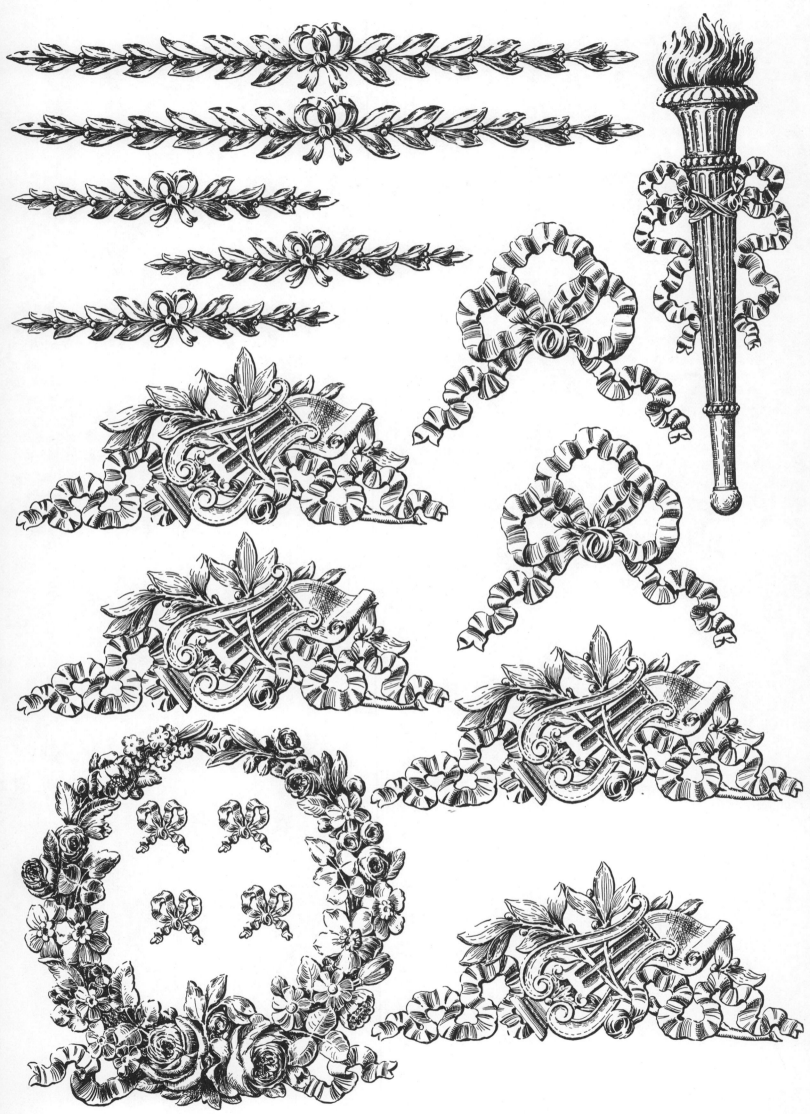

35

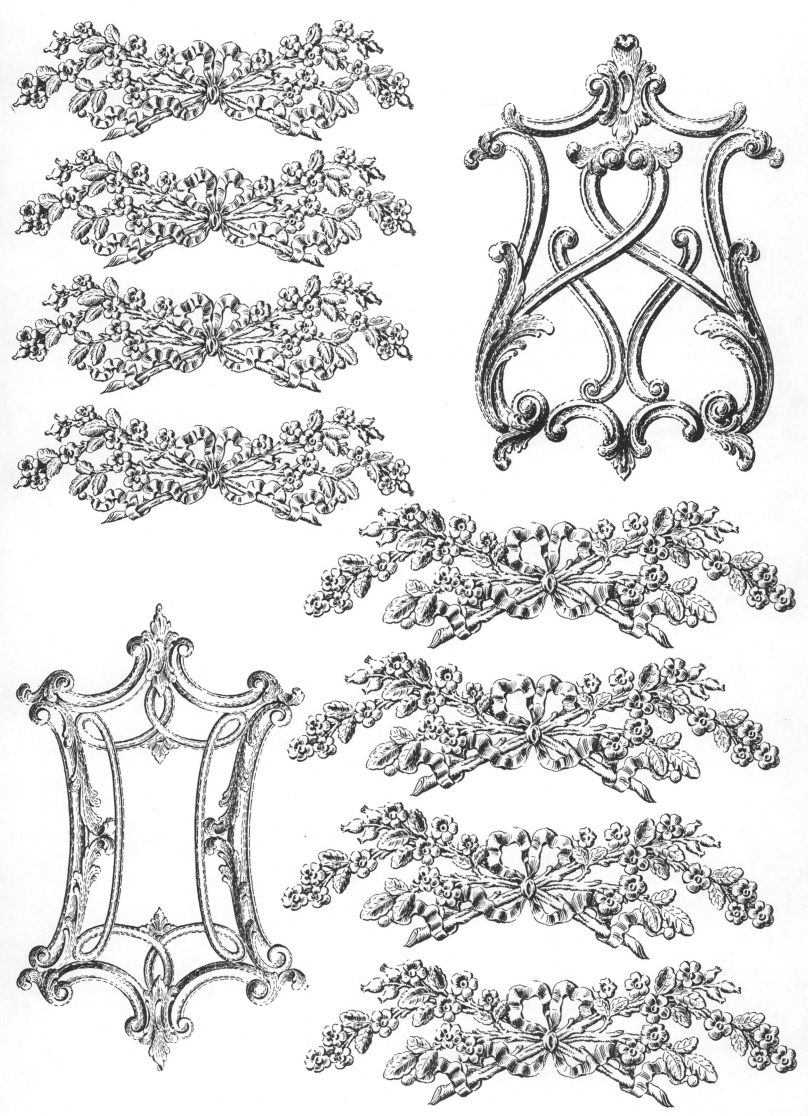

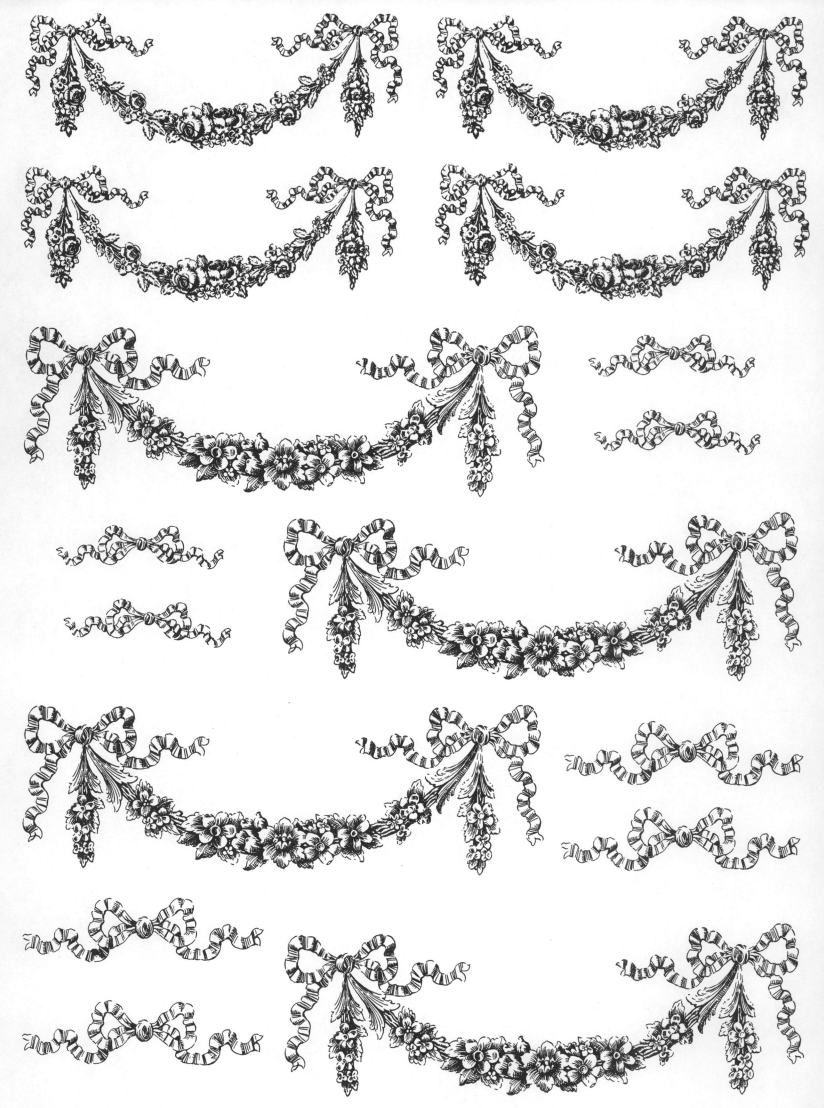

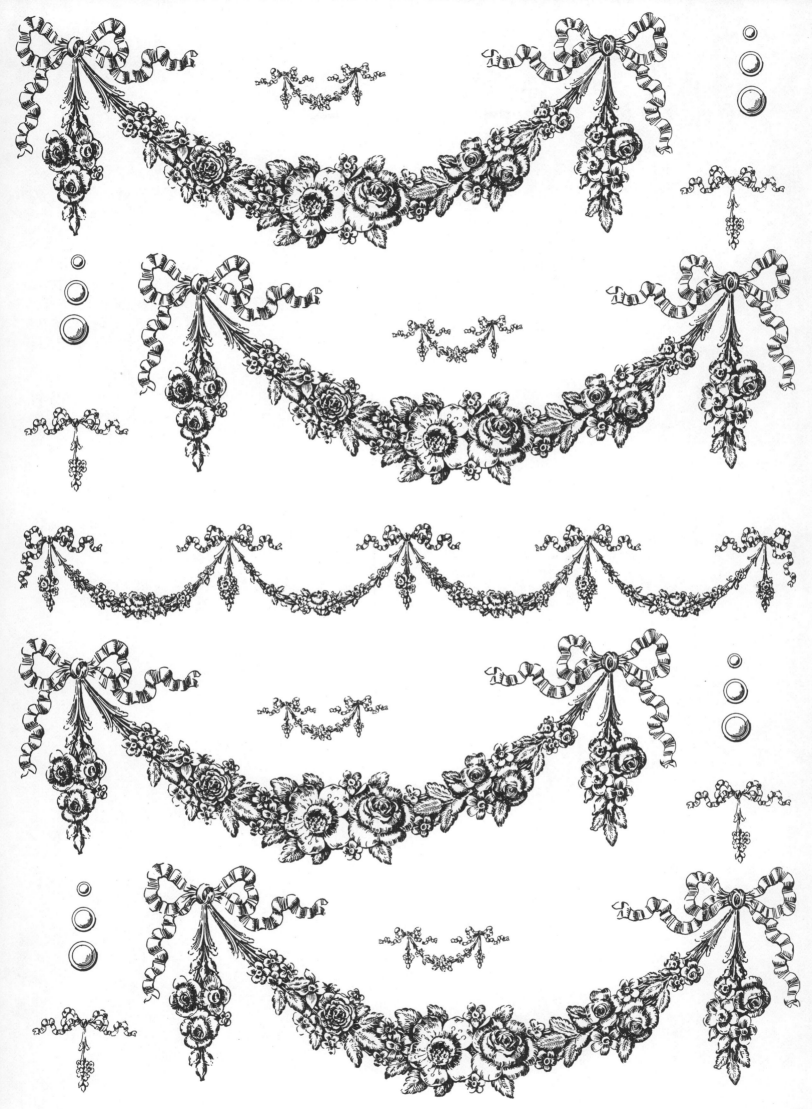

40

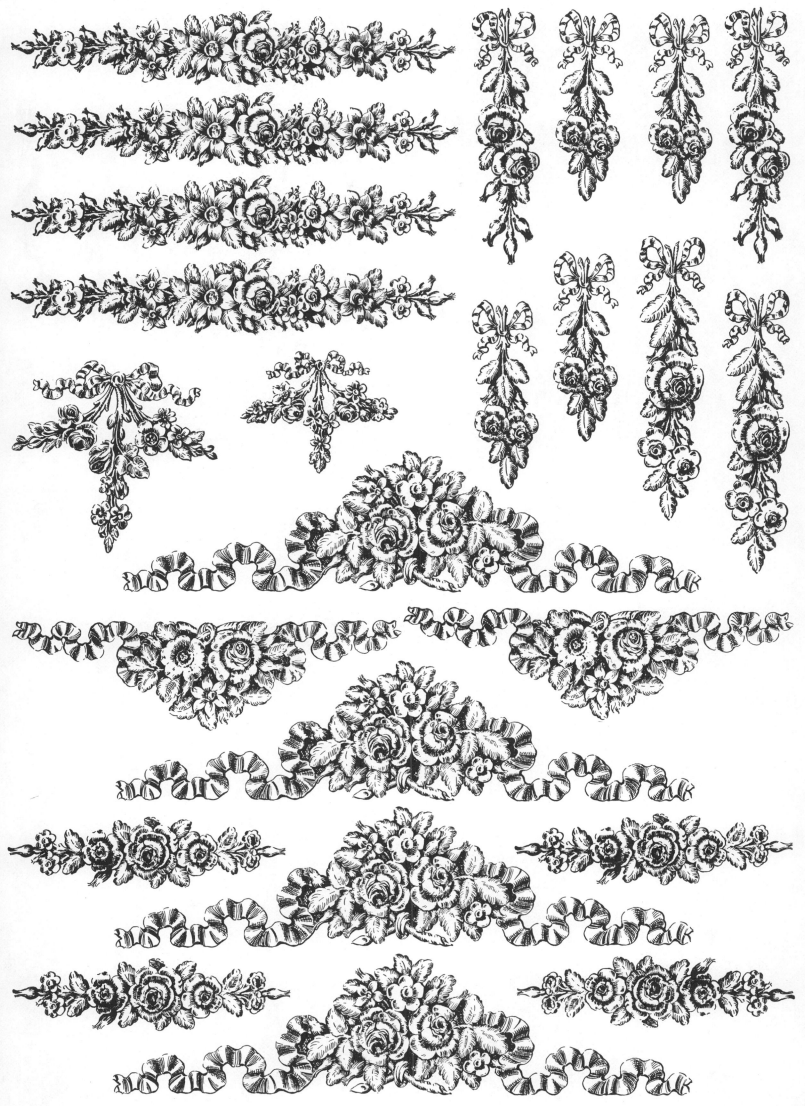

41

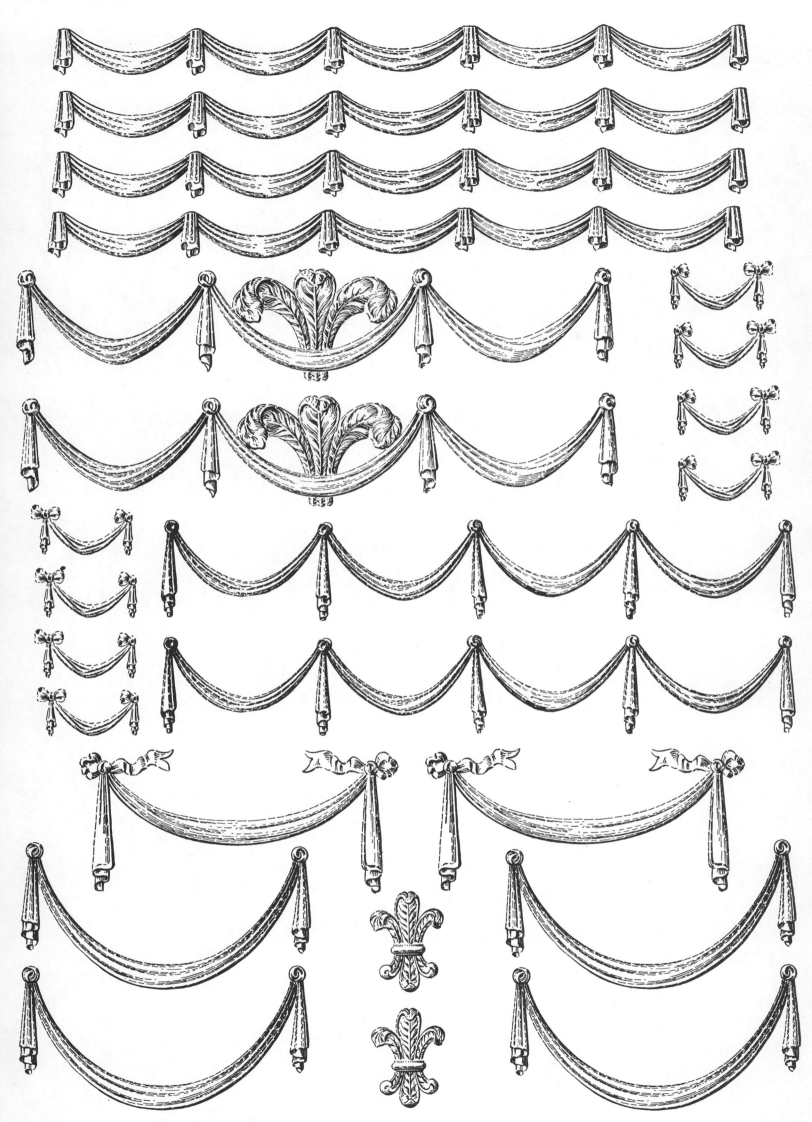

48

49

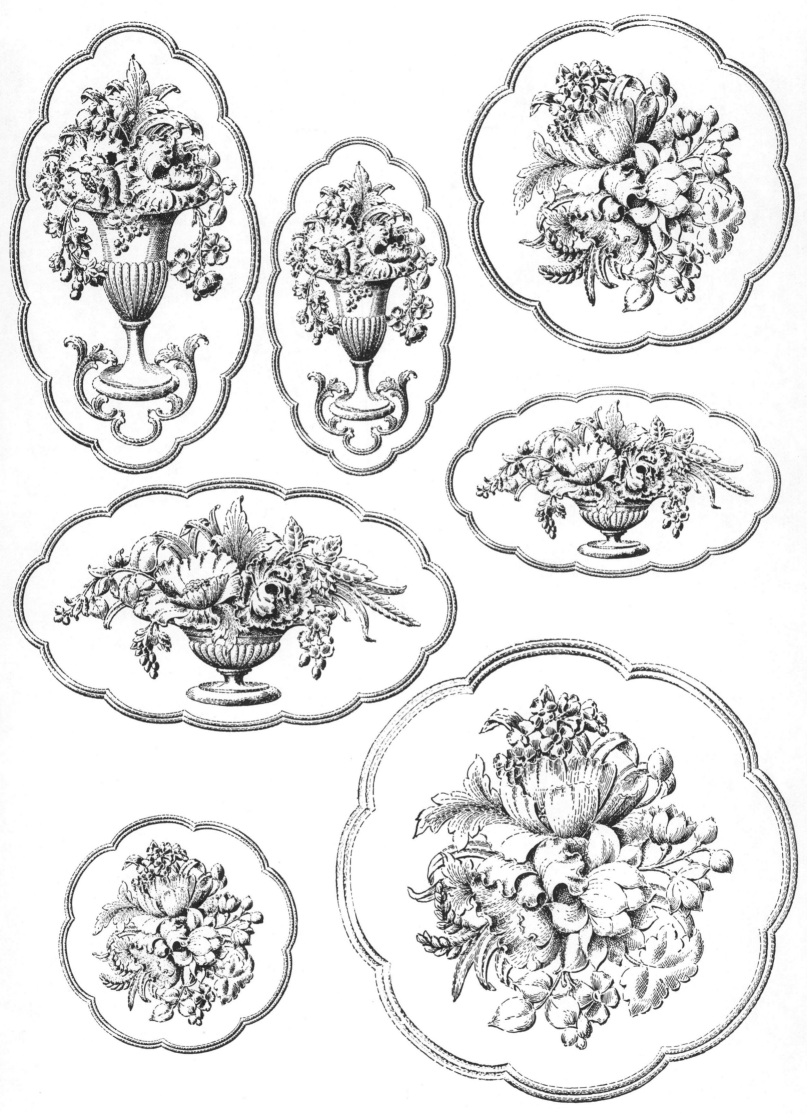

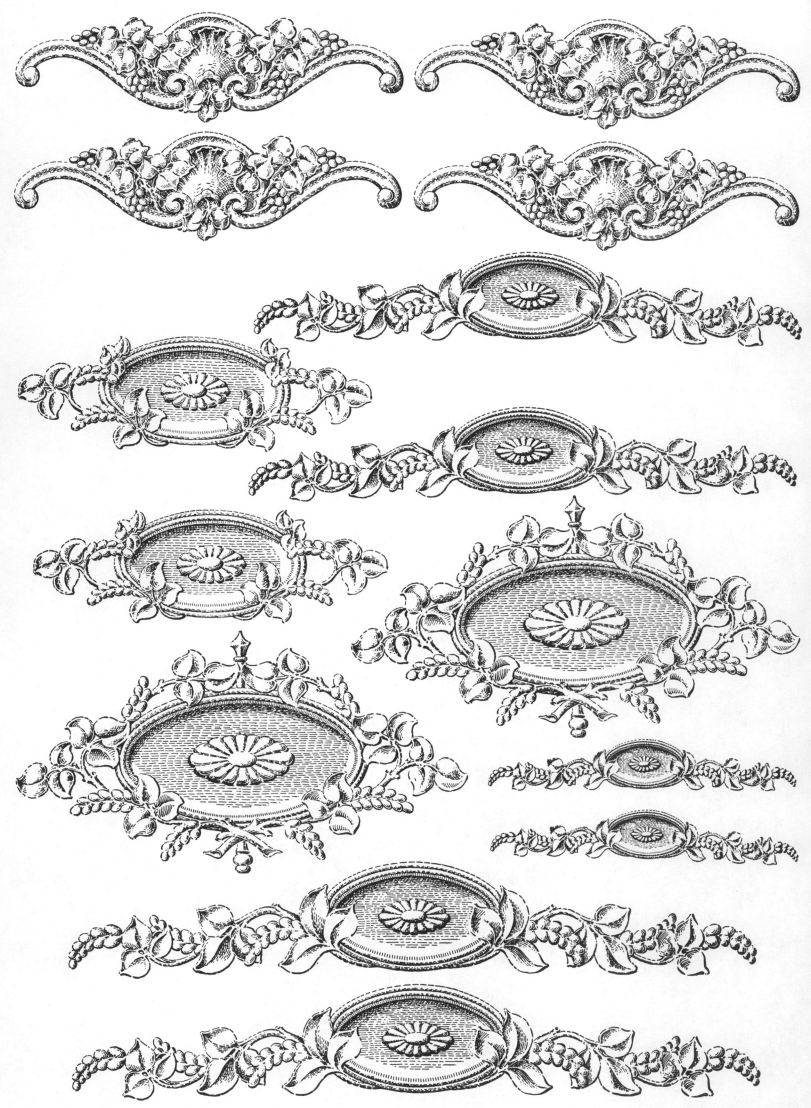

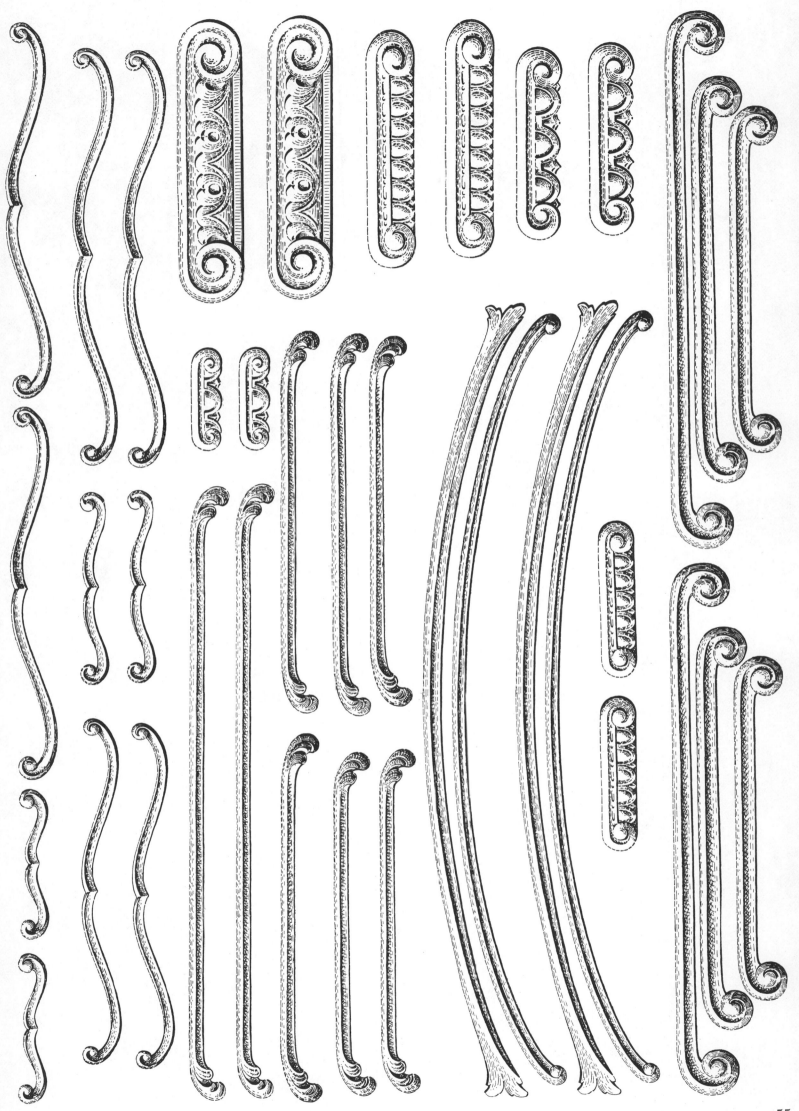

55

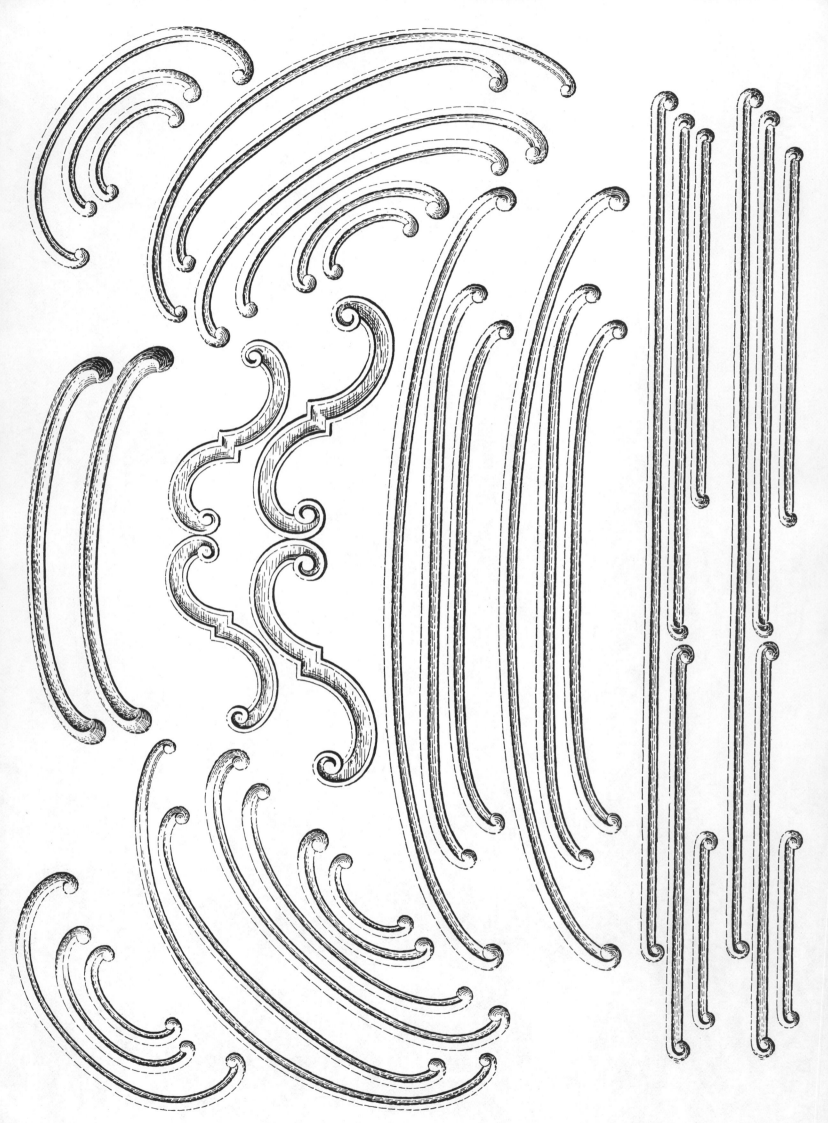

56

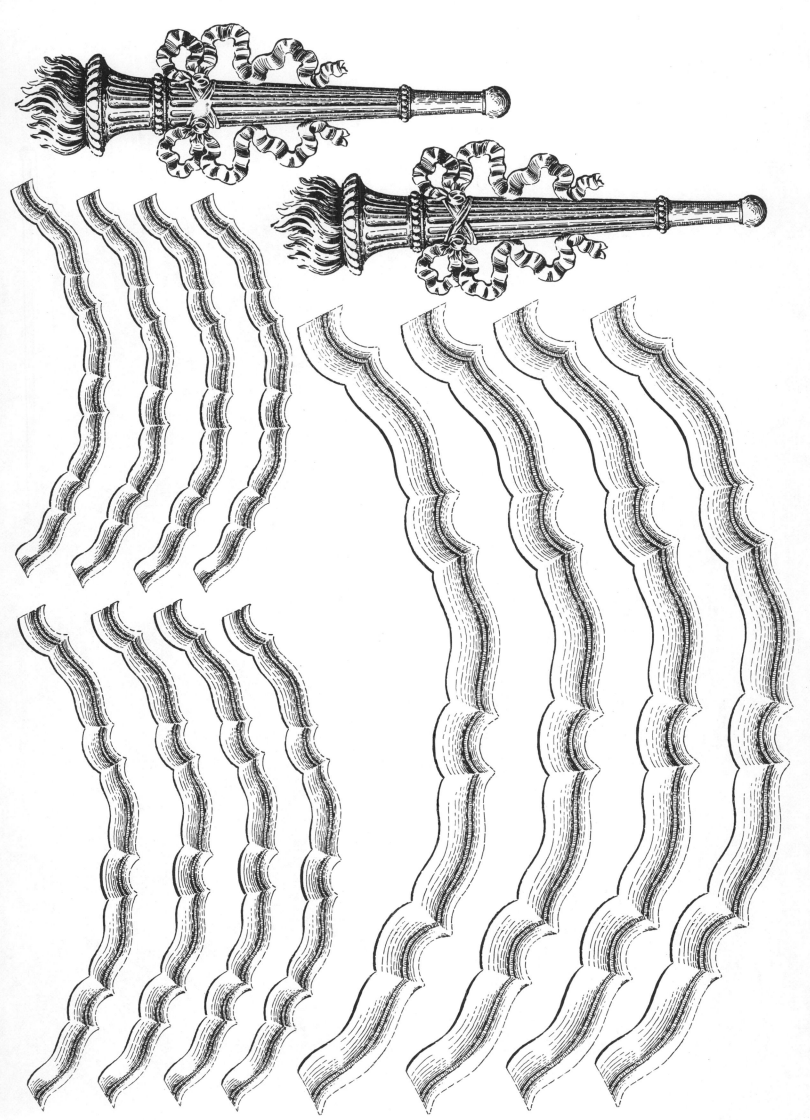

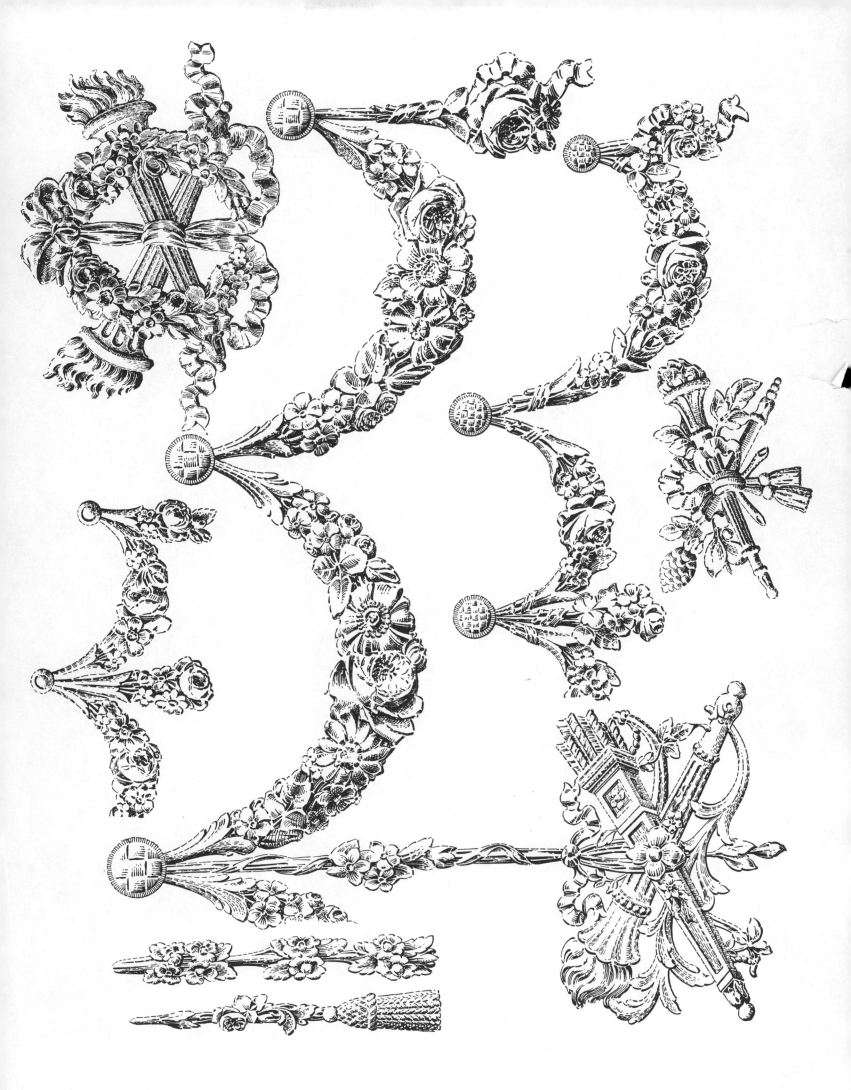